A LIBYAN ARTIST IN EXILE

Pauline's Place | 2010 - Ink on paper

A LIBYAN ARTIST IN EXILE
HASAN 'ALSATOOR' DHAIMISH
(1955-2016)

BY SHERIF DHAIMISH

This limited edition publication has been put together by
Pendle Press to accompany the 2021 exhibition, *Resistance,
Rebellion and Revolution*, which celebrates the life and work
of Libyan artist, Hasan Dhaimish (1955 – 2016).

Pendle Press

6 Gellatly Road, London, SE14 5TT, UK

First published in Great Britain in 2021

Designed by Luke Pajak

Text and images © Sherif Dhaimish

Images curated by Hanna Dhaimish

A catalogue record for this book is available from the British Library

ISBN - 978-1-8383-6930-9

Printed by Elma Basim, Turkey

www.pendle-press.co.uk

For my Mum, who is the soul of the family. And for Dad. The world ain't as pretty without you.

INTRODUCTION

There is often more than one side to every artist. Hasan was no different. As a satirist who lived in exile for most of his life, Hasan watched his home from afar and voiced an opinion through cartoons for four decades, under the pseudonym Alsatoor (The Cleaver).

But there was more to his artistry than satire. Much of Hasan's work was rooted in the culture he absorbed whilst living in Brierfield, a post-industrial town in Lancashire, northwest England.

From portraits of blues and jazz artists, to abstract scenes of African warriors and old street scenes of Libya, Hasan's work is an expression of his life as an exiled human.

THE EARLY YEARS

Hasan Mahmoud Dhaimish was born in the al-Shabi District of Benghazi, Libya, in 1955. Four years prior to his birth, Libya had become an autonomous Kingdom following hundreds of years of colonisation, first under the Ottomans (1551-1912), and then Italy (1912-1943). Libya's east where Hasan grew up, often referred to as Cyrenaica after the ancient Greek city of Cyrene, has often been on the receiving end of injustice; under Gaddafi, Benghazi's infrastructure was left to crumble, largely due to the city's history of rebellion to central rule in the western city of Tripoli. The Lion of the Desert himself, Omar Mukhtar, a Libyan icon of resistance and national hero to many, was from the east and fought against the Italians until his capture and execution in 1931.

When Hasan was born, King Idris was on the throne. He had shifted Libya's central power from today's capital Tripoli, to the eastern city of Tobruk which sits on the Mediterranean coast, 100 miles from the Egyptian border. Hasan's father, Sheikh Mahmoud Dhaimish, moved the family to Tobruk for two years, as he was appointed as the religious adviser and imam of the King.

Sheikh Mahmoud Dhaimish was a well respected man in eastern Libya who lived to the age of 97. He was a *hafiz* (someone who has memorised the Quran) by the age of 10, and went on to study at Egypt's al-Azhar University.

When he returned to Benghazi in the early 1950s, he helped establish the city's first radio station, where he would read sermons on air.

'I was politically aware at an early age, thanks to my father, who played a fundamental role in forming my ideas. I inherited the spirit of rebellion and not to be afraid to speak the truth and stand with the weak from him.'

As a young child, Hasan would watch his father draw pigeons on the roof tiles of their home where the family kept the birds. He would draw a single pigeon on each tile, while explaining his technique.

Sheikh Mahmoud also introduced Hasan to the famous Libyan artist, Mohammed al-Zawawi. They would study his techniques and discuss his satire, often bursting into fits of laughter. Noticing an eagerness to learn about art, his father was keen to share anything related to painting and politics, laying the foundations for Hasan's life ahead. He soon started drawing caricatures.

'At that time, I didn't realise that art chooses you, not the other way round.'

New suit for Eid | 1962 - Libya   *Afro!* | 1971 - Libya

'I remember my sister, who was also my best mate, getting engaged. I was angry about it, so I started drawing cartoons of her on the walls of our home. I never got in trouble, though. I think my dad saw I had talent. After that, I started drawing pictures of Gaddafi in my room. Soon afterwards, my brother-in-law found them and took them to local security forces. "Are you out of your goddamn mind?" I asked him. I was furious, but he said they had a good laugh at them, too, so there was nothing to worry about.'

At school he had started drawing classmates and teachers, much to the entertainment of those around him. Childhood friend Ahmed recalls:

'We had French lessons at high school. Our teacher was an Algerian gentleman who looked like a cartoon character - a thin moustache and prominent features. During the break of the class, Hasan would get up and draw the teacher on the chalkboard. When he would come back into the room, he'd look at the picture, rub everything off the board but leave the cartoon there.'

Art meant something to Hasan from a young age. It was a way to channel both his rebellious nature and curiosity. He was always reading the comics and magazines that were in his local library. Hasan would hide behind the bookshelves and read, laughing with tears rolling down his face. The mischievous nature of the characters he read about were an inspiration for his work later on.

He would also make regular trips to the cinema and wait for the animations that preceded the movie. This was his favourite part of the cinematic experience.

'My first attempt to draw was in primary school. In art class, I attempted to draw a Roman soldier as I was influenced by Italian movies like Hercules and Maciste.'

Sketching became an integral part of life for him, a second nature. When he started working at the local library, which doubled up as a publishing house, he would spend his time reading newspapers and engaging with the creatives who passed through, offering him a priceless education in journalism and politics, one no school could teach. He also played basketball for Benghazi's Al Ahli, the city's biggest club at the time. Another hobby was wandering the streets and souqs like al-Jarida and al-Zalam, where he would smell the scents emanating from the stores and admire the colourful fabrics being sold around him, all of which would play a role in his art later in life.

'I also used to spend time playing on the beach of al-Shabi. I would watch the ships while they disappeared beyond the horizon. I always wondered, where did they go? I was eager to know what existed beyond the sea. I used to imagine foreign cities and their people. The idea of travelling was stuck in my mind since childhood. I imagined myself building a boat and sailing away. Living on the edge was a part of me because of the sea.'

In the late 1960s, Hasan discovered music by tuning into shortwave radio. He would pick up the latest funk and soul from overseas and tape them on his reel-to-reel from his rooftop. Clad in dapper outfits consisting of flares, denim, and tailored shirts, and sporting a giant afro, he certainly looked the part.

Like all young Libyan men at the time, he had to do national service. He completed his stint under an invisible cloak, receiving little attention from generals and corporals. 'Dhaimish, eh? Where've you been hiding?' one commented whilst he was being discharged. That same cloak would come in useful over the next few decades, concealing his identity from Gaddafi's regime and the British Home Office. Hasan was about to leave Libya behind forever, and turn his paintbrush into the ultimate weapon of social and political dissidence.

Libyan National basketball team in Malta | 1972 - Libya

FROM BENGHAZI
TO BURNLEY

I'll tell you now and I'll tell you firmly
I don't never want to go to Burnley
What they do there don't concern me
Why would anybody make the journey?

- John Cooper Clarke

In 1975, aged 19, Hasan arrived in London with no intention of staying. Like many who left Libya in the 1970s, he believed Gaddafi would soon be deposed and that he would return to the warmth of North Africa. Stepping into cold England wasn't exactly what Hasan had envisioned - but the country soon became his playground.

He'd run wild at reggae festivals, discos and psychedelic parties, enjoying life without so much as a pittance in his pocket, while dodging all calls to return to Libya like bullets. His deportation was inevitable, but in the meantime, he drifted to Bradford, Yorkshire, and then made an impromptu journey to Burnley, Lancashire.

'I was in a cafe with some Libyan friends, and was introduced to a guy called Sa'ad. I asked him where he lived, and he replied, "Burnley". I'd never heard of the place, but after he assured me there was a college I could enrol in, I put my record player and rucksack in his Morris Minor and took off. Next thing I knew I had been in Burnley for 35 years.'

He'd gone from Benghazi to Burnley via Yorkshire. It was a case of life being stranger than fiction. It was here where he met Karen, who he married in 1979. Karen was born and raised in Brierfield, a small town next to Burnley, where she worked as a graphic artist.

'He was going to be deported on the Monday because they wouldn't grant him political asylum - the government sent a letter stating the time he had to be at Manchester Airport. So we got married on the Saturday just before. God knows what would've happened to him if he had been forced to return.'

Hasan was living like most 20somethings do - young, wild and free. But he lacked stability until he met Karen. He once said:

'She's been my rock since day one. I wouldn't have made anything of myself if it wasn't for her. She stuck by me through all the turbulence.'

And turbulence there was. Hasan was monitored closely by authorities due to his circumstances, but he now had a partner in crime. Karen helped Hasan learn English, something he did quickly. He would buy the Guardian daily and read it cover to cover, quizzing his wife on words he did not know, and then practised working them into sentences. They were a couple of young creatives whose love and friendship formed a bond that would last a lifetime.

Hasan's sister Amel visited and brought with her traditional Libyan outfits

THE BIRTH OF ALSATOOR

On a trip to London in 1980 with Karen, Hasan spotted an Arabic newsstand outside Earl's Court tube station.

'An orange magazine called Al-Jihad caught my eye from afar, so I went over, picked it up , and realised it was for the Libyan Opposition. It was about four pages with no contact information. I wanted to get involved with my cartoons. Luckily, the bright blue magazine next to it called Al-Sharq Al-Jadid had exactly the same articles inside, along with contact information. I bought both, took them back to Burnley with me and wrote to them. The only contact number I had belonged to my in-laws, Jack and Enid.'

A couple of weeks later, Enid arrived at the couple's flat. 'A Frenchman called for you and left his number'. Of course, the man wasn't French at all - he was Libyan, and it was Dr Mahmoud al-Maghrabi, the first prime minister of Libya after Gaddafi's 1969 coup.

Hasan began sending them caricatures of Gaddafi and his associates, which were received with adulation from readers and fellow members.

'Dr. Mahmoud al-Maghrabi was like a teacher to me. He taught me patience ... Another inspiring person was Fadel al-Masoudi [Libyan journalist and dissident], who taught me a lot about journalism and satire ... there are more, but these two figures left a mark on me.'

Initially, Hasan adopted the pseudonym 'Omran', but he soon dropped it, giving to the world 'Alsatoor' ('The Cleaver' in Arabic). Between 1980 and 1985, he produced cartoons for *Jihad*, a London-based magazine, and also began attending rallies including the infamous event where PC Yvonne Fletcher was shot dead outside the Libyan embassy on St James's Square, London, in April 1984. As the only Libyan for miles around in Burnley, Alsatoor was able to operate covertly and blend into his new hometown as best a foreigner could. He was well aware of the dangers his work posed for him and his family back in Libya, but also for his family in the UK.

Between 1980 and 1987, Amnesty International reported a series of assassinations of 'stray dogs' by the dictator's international death squads. 'It is the Libyan people's responsibility to liquidate the scum who are distorting Libya's image abroad,' Gaddafi warned dissidents.

As his work began to grow in popularity, Alsatoor remained an anonymous enigma within and outside Libyan borders; a mysterious persona that was the product of a slick pseudonym and a keen awareness of the risks involved.

20   *Sherif aged one reading* Alsatoor | 1989

Sheikh Khalifa bin Hamad al-Thani of Qatar and King Fahd of Saudi Arabia | Taken from *Alraai Alakhar* - September 1990

EXILE IN THE 1980S

Six months after the shooting at the embassy in 1984, Hasan became a father to his first daughter, Zahra. He was working at Carlo's Italian restaurant in Colne at the time. Hasan had embraced life in northwest England, as the distance between himself and Libya continued to grow.

He didn't join any other anti-regime movements, as he was convinced that they were unable to change or effect serious change in Libya. Instead, he had established Alsatoor as an independent voice. As the Libyan Opposition entered a phase of stagnation, Alsatoor began publishing his work independently.

Carlo's restaurant in Colne with Angelo and the late Maurizio | 1990   *Near Pendle Hill* | 1979

'I knew then that cartoons were a powerful tool, but they had a stronger impact than I had ever imagined.'

Burnley and Pendle once stood at the heart of Lancashire's cotton production and engineering industries. In the 1980s, parts of northern England had become an industrial graveyard under Thatcher. Pakistani immigrants who came to reboot the textile industry during the 1970s and 80s were living in the area, but there was a general lack of integration, an issue that still exists today. Mix all of this together, and you have one of Britain's most deprived areas, albeit surrounded by beautiful countryside.

Hasan was never victim to race attacks, but he often spoke of the systematic racism that existed at the time. Intimidating immigration officers would often pay him random visits, even after he was married. Before that, he was treated with hostility by authorities despite the obvious danger of returning to Libya. Saying that, it never phased him to the point that he stopped living his life and making friends in the area.

Away from Alsatoor, Hasan had an eclectic group of friends. There was Ivan* who shared Hasan's passion for reggae; Paul 'Harry Hippie', a rogue mechanic who lived up the road; Jerome the jeweller; Maurizio, Pino, Nuncia, Simon, Aldo and Mario from Carlo's; Manfredo the barber; Groovy Chris; Andy Ford the photographer; Cerise, Roy, Frank and Siobhan from college; Paul the potterer; Simon and John; Faust the magician. There were many more who came and went over the years.

Hasan's artistic flare was about to transform, as he unshackled himself from the caricature.

*Hasan and Ivan once claimed to have seen a UFO over Todmorden, West Yorkshire, back in the 1980s. They weren't the only people to have made a sighting in the area around that time.

EDUCATION, EDUCATION AND ARTISTIC EXPLORATION

In the early 1990s, Hasan passed his driving test, which opened a world of possibilities and gave him the confidence to return to studies. In 1991, he enrolled on a computer course at Nelson and Colne College.

'I was in a classroom in front of an Amiga computer. Everyone was typing while I just stared at the screen not understanding what I was required to do. I found a program with a brush and colours, so I started to draw.'

This is how Hasan kept himself occupied for the first few classes. When Will Barton, the class teacher, pulled Hasan to one side, he thought he was getting kicked out of class for not following the task. But instead, Will offered Hasan a letter of acceptance to the college, and as a result he received a grant from Lancashire County Council to help him through his studies.

'I was scared at first - I didn't know what would be required of me. I could draw simple caricatures, but studying fine art is something else.'

Shortly afterwards, he was outside Carlo's - the Italian restaurant where he'd been working for the last ten years - having a cigarette, when Will from the college walked past. He told him his future lay elsewhere, not waiting tables.

'His words struck me like a thunderbolt.'

Hasan was more motivated than ever. He returned to college, finished his A-Levels and then went on to Bradford University to study a BA in Illustration.

After the birth of his and Karen's third child, Hanna in 1993 - sister to Zahra and Sherif (born in 1988), he was close to graduation after cramming six years' worth of studies into just four. His time at college and university was spent around other creatives, which influenced his own artistic style. He began experimenting with video and painting more and more.

'I moved away from satire and switched to painting, using music of black Americans and their social history as inspiration.'

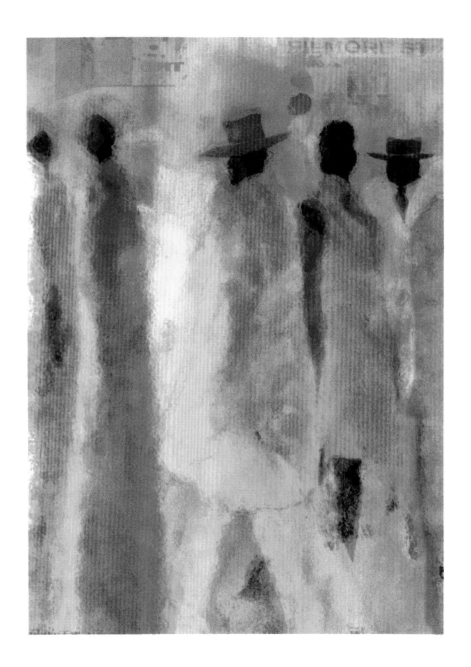

Some forms Hasan explored were more experimental than others. One phase he had was using clear masks and heads as a subject. He would fill them with objects, paint them in fluorescent colours to then hold them up to a UV light and film them with jazz in the background. It was art Hasan could really indulge himself in. He was dabbling in avant-garde - a piece his children remember vividly consisted of their two goldfish* swimming around a glass head to High Speed Chase by Miles Davis. Hypnagogic.

Has, as he was known among peers, began teaching in 1995 at Nelson and Colne College. He soon became popular for his approach to art and curricula. Background music never ceased to resound and turn students on to his waves of artistic experimentation.

He'd paint to the sounds of musicians like Miles Davis, Thelonious Monk, and Dexter Gordon, or Blind Wille Johnson and Skip James, bringing jazz and the blues to life through his artwork. Black culture became the backbone for his work - he swore by Paul Oliver's *Story of the Blues*, and Iceberg Slim's *Pimp* and *Trick Baby*.

In 2002, he joined the social site Deviant Art under the username 'Alsature'. His work was far removed from the satire he was producing elsewhere. It was a space to experiment and create art for a different audience. It was a breathing space away from the political sphere full of funk and colour. In typical fashion, Hasan lost the password around 2010, and wasn't able to log into his account again, so his flow of work comes to an abrupt end there, but it's still available to view online.

History of the Blues part 1 | 2010 - Pen on paper

*They both lived to the age of 23.

Da Vinci once said: 'Art is never finished, only abandoned.' Some of Hasan's paintings have been painted on top of others. Pentimenti adds a dimension to his work that wasn't always intentional; he would often paint over his least favourite canvas when nothing else was available. It added texture – a layering that he first experimented with as a student.

He began scavenging detritus on the streets of Pendle, looking for obscure objects to incorporate into his art – old sacks, fishing wire … Old posters around town would always catch his eye, making him stop the car and rip off layers to attach and paint over his previous work.

In the early 2000s Hasan found the aforementioned *The Story of the Blues* by Paul Oliver in a skip near his Brierfield home. This book changed his life. Oliver's pictorial history of the 20th century's most influential musical form introduced him to artists who pioneered the Mississippi Delta sound. Hasan had gone back in time; his haphazard genre-hopping matched his approach to almost everything.

The blues was from the soul, and the lyrics touched him deeply; so much so that he'd imprint them onto his paintings and sketches. This culture that seemed so far removed from his life in Brierfield was one he identified with. It was the sadness, the disconnectedness and expatriatism that drew him.

The Soul of a Man by Blind Willie Johnson (1930)

Won't somebody tell me, answer if you can!
Want somebody tell me, what
is the soul of a man
I'm going to ask the question, answer if you can
If anybody here can tell me,
what is the soul of a man?
I've traveled in different countries, I've traveled foreign lands
I've found nobody to tell me,
what is the soul of a man

Many of Hasan's friendships were built on music. There must be hundreds of mixtapes out there that he put together for people, scribbling cartoons on the covers.

Before he found jazz, his musical taste revolved around reggae and dub, which was prestigious in West Yorkshire, home to some of the nation's most devastating sound systems.

'I used to stand there and the speakers would vibrate my whole body. "Wob wob wob" would ripple through you until you couldn't take anymore.'

From the rugged sounds of The Beastie Boys and Public Enemy to the multifaceted samplers De La Soul, A Tribe Called Quest and Gang Starr, hip hop's influence took hold of Hasan's work in the early 90s, which was well-rooted in the funk and soul he grew up on. Producer Easy Mo Bee's contribution to Miles Davis' Doo Bop album combined the soft synth, snapping snare and fluid basslines of hip hop pioneers of the time, merged with the timeless sound of Miles's trumpet. The album was a stepping stone, perhaps even the gatekeeper to a boundless network of musical exploration for Hasan.

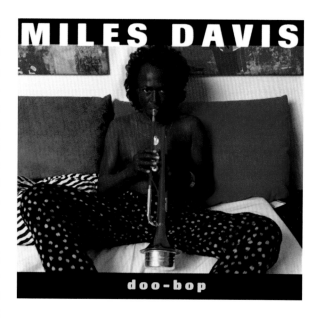

Although the album was released in 1992, it resonated in his work right through the 90s. Vibrant images depicting movement and chaos dominated his portfolio. The satire was always there, Alsatoor never slept; but his art really came to life away from politics. Through studying A-Levels and a degree, and then becoming a graphics teacher, art allowed Hasan to escape the torment of exile.

In the same year as Doo Bop, another album would be released that held a special place in Hasan's heart: Secret Story by Pat Metheny. This world jazz album drew influence from various eras and countries including Cambodia, Japan, Eastern Europe and North America; an eclecticism Hasan found identifiable in his own work, and perhaps even himself.

As a Libyan living in exile, England had become his home away from home. But there was always the feeling of being in transit, belonging to neither here nor there. Music helped bridge the gap between head and heart.

THE DIGITAL AGE

At the turn of the millennium came the rise of the internet - a pivotal change that would make Alsatoor's work globally accessible. He was commissioned some illustrations for a software and web development company based in Pendle called Subnet, and that's where he got his first email address. At the time, around 2000, he didn't have access to the internet at home.

'Someone called me from Subnet, and told me I'd received my first email after they had created a website for my paintings. It was from Dr Ibrahim Ighneiwa, who asked me for permission to add my site to libyawatanona.com, which I accepted.'

Hasan then got online and soon realised the potential of Alsatoor. He spent hours alone listening to jazz and classical music. They were his companions on the long British winter nights spent in front on the screen.

'I loved jazz because of its melody and the conditions from which it appeared. I identified with the history of black people in America, based on my own suffering and persecution.'

Hasan's studying didn't stop. He would read up on artists, taking a particular interest in Henri de Toulouse-Lautrec, Pablo Picasso, Jean-Michel Basquiat and Keith Haring, all of whom influenced his own work.

The Colonel | One of Alsatoor's digital cartoons of Muammar Gaddafi, first published on Libya Watonona, 2003

'Happy?' | Gaddafi's former state protocol secretary Nuri al-Mismari and the colonel. Watonona, 2003

I KILL 'IRAQI' CHILDREN   I KILL 'LIBYAN' CHILDREN

توني بلير يعد الزعيم الليبي بأسلحة حديثة

يطلق لندن هذا؟

(على ضوء انعقاد المؤتمر الوطني للمعارضة الليبية)

After the teaching day was finished, Has became Alsatoor. He would glue himself to his desk, observing Arabic news stations that were picked up from an array of sketchy satellite dishes on the side of the house.

Illegal access to Libyan news channels revolutionised Alsatoor's work, as he could now rip sound and video straight from the TV and manipulate them. He would watch the Libyan national Al-Jamahiriya channel, granting him access to Gaddafi's rambled speeches.

'It was an effective method in my fight against him. I would get complaints from Libyan authorities on my YouTube channel later on, but it didn't stop me. I was constantly being targeted, as I never set myself limits. People would complain that Alsatoor had exceeded the limits of morality, and they demanded I deleted my insulting cartoons of Gaddafi and his family, but they were to no avail.'

In 2003, Libya Al Mostakbal was launched - a pro-democracy Libya news site run by Hasan Al-Amin. This provided another platform for Alsatoor, with Libyans all over the world becoming followers of his work.

During the 2000s, Hasan's family were harassed online via Facebook and email hackings, and threats were sent directly to his children. But none of this dissuaded nor frightened Alsatoor; if anything it spurred him on.

Former British PM Tony Blair and Gaddafi, a selection | 2004   39

Around the same time, the 'New Libya' had reopened its doors to the West, and hopes of the regime's collapse seemed more distant than ever. It emerged that MI6 and the CIA were exchanging details on dissidents for extraordinary renditions. Photos of Tony Blair shaking hands with Gaddafi were a bleak image, but the online response to his work spurred him on.

In the years building up to the Libyan revolution, Hasan published his work online through his own blog: alsature. wordpress.com. Just like when he started publishing works independently in print in the 1980s, it was here that he had full editorial control. This, however, was on a global scale. His work was often so offensive and relentless that other outlets like Libya Al Mostakbal refused to place them on the site.

It was a tough time for Hasan. He battled with depression and the loss of his father in 2009 drew him into a dark place. He had been away from Libya, his home, his family, for 34 years and there was no sign of change anytime soon due to the path he had set out on, and the real dangers that existed for dissidents stepping foot in Gaddafi's Libya. But despite everything, Hasan was prolific with his paintbrush, both as Alsatoor and on the canvas.

ليبيا الغد

REVOLUTION

In January 2011, the Arab Spring began to sweep across North Africa and the Middle East. People were demanding change in countries that had autocratic rulers for decades. Libya broke out into civil war in February, changing the country's future forever.

Alsatoor was working at his home in Brierfield from the moment he returned from teaching at his new workplace, Craven College, Skipton, until he went to bed in the early hours. He would sketch whilst on the phone, watching TV and researching online. His blog was overloaded with posts, photos and information people were sharing with him. He was doing his best to operate as a pro-revolution news outlet, and it worked, as shortly afterwards the newly-established Libya Al-Ahrar TV asked him to join them in Doha, Qatar, and work for them.

Alsatoor, hesitant to leave his job and wife behind, knew this was his calling - his chance to join like-minded Libyans and have his work broadcasted. Like many others involved in the channel, he worked around the clock to deliver news to the masses around the world who were following Libya's fight for freedom.

In October 2011, Gaddafi was captured and killed in Sirte and the whole world watched. Alsatoor was, like many, in a state of ecstasy; the man he had watched and

observed from a distance, the dictator who had been the subject of his work, the source of his woes, the reason he left his family behind in Libya, and the reason he left his family behind in the UK, too, was now dead.

44

Tributes to the fallen. Tariq al-Drissi, Tawfik Ben Saud & Sami Elkawafi | 2014

Former US Ambassador to Libya, Deborah Jones | 2013 (top)   *Former Libyan PM Ali Zeidan* | 2013 (bottom)

The work didn't stop there for Alsatoor; if anything, the new state of chaos in Libya was far more demanding due to the political complexities. He began churning out cartoons, criticising political players from all angles. The form of his work had changed, but his message had not - no one escaped Alsatoor.

Even though Hasan had pledged to stop drawing Gaddafi once his regime fell, his daily publications continued to criticise Libya's debilitated political landscape, and those who chose to enter it. From those in parliament, Western diplomats and politicians, to religious figures and journalists. As sociopolitical issues flared up across the country, Alsatoor watched on like a hawk.

Subsequent years saw a string of events rip Benghazi apart - the attack on the US consulate resulting in the death of Ambassador Christopher Stevens, and a long string of assassinations of civil rights activists and army officers. Alsatoor would always honour the fallen through his art published online, expressing solidarity with his country people whose lives were lost in the fight for freedom.

Doha sucked the creative spark from Hasan; he tried painting in his hotel room where he lived, but he claimed that Qatar provided him with little inspiration. He wanted to return to the UK, but he gave into the demand for Alsatoor, and in reality the money was too good to turn down.

During his final years, his artistic flair was subsumed by Libya's poisonous political landscape. But this could also be considered Alsatoor's golden era - Libyans could freely discuss politics and air views across social media, making his work live, interactive, relevant. He corresponded with people online, and surrounded himself with those he respected and trusted. One of those was Omar El Keddi, a Libyan writer who many believed to be Alsatoor. He had the following to say about Alsatoor:

'He was a wonderful, talented man. I started giving him ideas for his cartoons, and he often put my name under Alsatoor. Many people started thinking I was him! I remember when I published my own name after the revolution, and Alsatoor's response was, "OK great, they'll kill you, not me." I miss him so much.'

In 2014, Hasan left Doha after three years and returned to the UK. Libya Al Ahrar TV had become a mouthpiece for Qatar and Alsatoor didn't suit the outlet. He continued producing work, but was in limbo as to whether he should return to teaching or focus on Alsatoor. The latter seemed like the most sensible option as the momentum was already there.

A year later he went to Amman, Jordan, to work for the newly-founded news station, 218TV. He didn't want to leave his family behind for a second time and return to the Middle East, although Amman seemed like a place that offered more to Hasan than Doha ever could. Sadly, he fell ill while working there and had to return to the UK in the following year.

He passed away on 12th August 2016 aged 60.

LEGACY

Hasan never chose to integrate with the Libyan dias-
pora. This wasn't because he was antisocial or didn't
belong, but because he was an anomaly, a deviant, an
eccentric. He was the buzzing fly Gaddafi had failed to
swat. With the advent of social media, Hasan aroused
laughter, hatred, and controversy amongst his followers.
The passion he had for the cause he'd fought for during
his early days as an asylum seeker in England lived on,
and his flame continued to burn.

His ambition was always to promote education, crea-
tivity, and individuality amongst youth, and he fulfilled
this. First and foremost, he was a teacher; he was a black
sheep in all the right ways, and anyone who spent time
with him became enlightened somehow, whether in their
knowledge of art, music, politics, football, or Libya.

Truth be told, Alsatoor became a burden to Hasan. All
Hasan wanted to do was paint under the blue skies of the
Mediterranean and the grey clouds of Lancashire; but
his selflessness and desire for a free Libya were stronger
than his desire to paint.

NOTE FROM THE AUTHOR

One of the best pieces of advice my dad ever gave me was: 'Just because I'm your dad doesn't mean I'm right.' He taught me to think critically about the world around me.

Working on this project has been enlightening. It has brought me closer to people who knew my dad and those who cared about him - from childhood friends, colleagues and former students at the colleges he taught.

Alsatoor was a persona that was kept away from me and my family growing up. I sort of knew what he was up to in the attic of our first family home in Brierfield and in the study at our next home. I knew he was drawing cartoons, but he was always doing that. He'd be on the phone while drawing - I knew when the person was boring him because he'd be drawing me and writing notes whilst holding a conversation.

His satire was stark, honest and often offensive. There aren't many straight talking cats like him about. No nonsense. His art was joyful. A real treat on the eye, and what I would consider an expression of who he really was. He had the funk.

He was an enigma to many, but it wasn't that way for me. He was my best mate. And this is all just a tribute to him to ensure his legacy lives on. He was a modest man who stuck to his principles and saw value in exposing the truth, and the world deserves to know his story. So I'll do my best to keep on telling it.

Rest in peace, Dad.

Sherif Dhaimish

SELECTED WORKS

Night In Tunisia | Unknown - Ink on paper

Water No Get Enemy | 2014 - Ink & oil pastel

Jam Session 1932 │ 2010 - Ink & watercolour

Everything Scatter | 2010 - Watercolour

Rankett Blues | 2007 - Pencil, watercolour & pastel

Untitled 1 | Unknown - Ink

Bamako Market | Unknown - Acrylic on card

Untitled | 2001 - Watercolour & pen 69

70   *The Funeral of Leroy Carr* | 2008 - Charcoal

Tunga Magni | 2008 - Ink on paper

Me and The Devil Blues | 2006 - Mixed media

Vibe PM | 2009 - Ink & watercolour

Down Here on the Ground | Unknown - Ink

Medina | 2009 - Acrylic on canvas

SKETCHES OF LIBYA

طرابلس هوتيل و مسرح ودان 1935

THE CORNER HOUSE

BIRRA OEA

زوارة 1913

درنة القديمة
1945

Tripoli in Springtime | Unknown